Card
Games

Card Games

John Cornelius

p

This is a Parragon Book
This edition published in 2001

Parragon
Queen Street House
4 Queen Street
Bath BA1 1HE, UK

ISBN: 0-75256-345-9

Produced by Haldane Mason, London

Printed in China

Produced by Haldane Mason, London

Acknowledgements
Art Director: Ron Samuels
Editor: Charles Dixon-Spain
Design: Zoë Mellors

Contents

Start Here

Welcome to the colourful and exciting world of card games! In this book you will find clear explanations of thirty-five games, giving you the essential know-how for many more. Card games tend to come in 'families' with lots of variations. Once you know the basic game, it's easy to play the others. There are games here for you to play on your own, with one other person, or with three or more. In each section the games gradually become more complex.

THE BASICS

A standard pack of cards has 52 cards, divided into 4 suits of 13 cards each. The suits are clearly marked by their symbols – hearts, clubs, diamonds and spades. Each card has a value. Ace is either top or bottom, depending on the game. Then, from the top, king, queen, jack, and the number cards from 10 to 2. There is an extra card, not used in all games, the joker. He normally beats everything.

At the start of almost every game, the pack is shuffled, so that the cards are thoroughly mixed, and then cut. This means that a player other than the one who shuffled lifts around half of the shuffled stack and swaps the two halves around, so that the upper half becomes the lower half.

Card games are international, but beware – often there are differences between the British and the American versions of a game with the same name. Some games with the same name are quite different in the two countries. Even within a single country, there can be variations of the same game. It doesn't really matter. Just make sure that anyone you play with is playing to the same rules as you.

Most card games can be used for gambling, and some are designed for it. Currency can be anything from plastic tokens to the real thing – whatever it is, don't bet beyond your ability to pay.

Note of Apology:

In this book, players are referred to as 'he'. This is used as an abbreviation of 'he or she' and is not in any way meant to exclude female players from the pleasure of card-playing. Also, Bridge is not included here because the rules and methods of play would fill a short book like this many times over.

All 52 cards in the pack (plus the two jokers) ordered top to bottom, with aces low.

Technical Terms

Ace High: Ace is top scoring card (and Ace Low is the opposite).

Ante: The amount each player pays into the Pool at the beginning of a gambling game.

Available Card: In Patience, a card that can be used in play (depending upon the rules of the game).

Building Up: In Patience, laying cards in ascending order of value on top of a Foundation Card. Building Down is laying them in descending order.

Chips: Tokens used in gambling games; different chips can be given different values.

Column: Cards laid on the table in a vertical line (top of one meets or overlaps bottom of another).

Court Cards: Kings, queens and jacks.

Deal: Pass out cards to players. The dealer holds the pack face down, takes from the top, and goes clockwise around the players. Most deals are one card at a time to each player, but this can vary.

Deck: Another word applied to the Pack.

Discard: In some games, this means playing a card of no value in the game, when the player cannot Follow Suit or play a Trump; in others, it means playing a card to the Waste Pile.

File: In Patience, a column in the Layout, with cards overlapping, but with their suits and Pip Values visible. Files are built up towards the player.

Flush: A Hand of cards all of the same suit.

Follow Suit: To play a card of the same suit as the first card played in a Trick.

Foundation Card: In Patience, a card laid down on which other cards are built up or down. They are normally aces or kings.

Hand: The cards held by a player during the game. In Patience, it can also be any cards which have not been dealt out (also known as the Stock).

Honours: Ace, king, queen and jack of the Trump suit.

Layout: The arrangement of cards in Patience games. Also called the Tableau.

Lead: To play first to a Trick. Also the card played first (Lead Card).

Meld: A set of three or more of a kind, e.g. either all kings, or all hearts (but these must be in sequence of Pip Value with no gaps).

Pack: The full set of 52 cards (or 53 when the joker is included).

Packet: Part of a Pack.

Pair: Two cards of the same kind, e.g. two sevens.

Pass: To miss a turn.

Pip Value: The number of pips on a number card (e.g. a nine has nine pips).

Pool: The cash or gambling Chips staked in a game, usually placed in the middle of the table. Also called the 'kitty' or the 'pot'.

Plain Card: Card not of the Trump suit.

Play: To play a card is to take it from your hand and use it in the game.

Rank: The value of a card.

Redeal: In Patience, using the cards from the Waste Pile to deal again, when the Stock is used up.

Renege: To fail to follow suit in a game where following suit is not obligatory. Often confused with Revoke.

Revoke: To play an incorrect card, normally by failing to follow suit when able to, in a game when following suit is obligatory if you can do so. Often confused with Renege.

Round: This is complete when each player has played his cards in any Trick.

Row: In Patience, a line of cards placed side by side (suit and Pip Value must always be visible if the cards overlap).

Rubber: A set of games, especially in Whist and Bridge.

School: A group of players playing for money.

Sequence: The order in which the cards run, from high to low, or the other way round.

Singleton: A single card of any suit.

Stock: The cards remaining after dealing, sometimes also called the Hand.

Tableau: Another word for the Layout.

Talon: Another word for Waste Pile.

Trick: The cards played by all the players in a round, one from each. It is normally won, or taken, by the player who played the highest card in the leading suit, or the highest Trump.

Trumps: Cards of a chosen suit that outrank all cards in other suits during the game. Trumping (sometimes referred to as Ruffing in Whist and Bridge) is playing a Trump Card.

Waste Pile: Cards turned up in the course of playing Patience that are not available for play according to the rules of the game. Also sometimes referred to as the Talon.

Wild Card: A card which a player can use to represent any other card (within the rules of the game).

♣ Games for One

In a way, these games do have two players – you and the pack. The aim is to beat the cards. When you do, it's a great satisfaction. These games are all forms of Patience, also called Solitaire. You need a good-sized table to out lay the cards, although it is possible to find special Patience packs in a smaller size. And of course, in these games it's impossible to cheat without being found out!

Accordion

AIM OF THE GAME: To be left with all the cards in one pile.

HOW TO PLAY: Use the standard 52-card pack. Deal out all the cards, face-up, in a single
   row, not overlapping.

The cards can then be moved as follows:
1. Move a card on to the card on its left, if it is the same suit or the same pip value.
2. Move a card on to the card third from the left, if it is the same suit or same pip value.

   After making a move, look to see if additional moves are possible. When cards are
stacked, move the whole stack, according to the value or suit of the uppermost card.

   You win if you finish with all the cards in one pile.

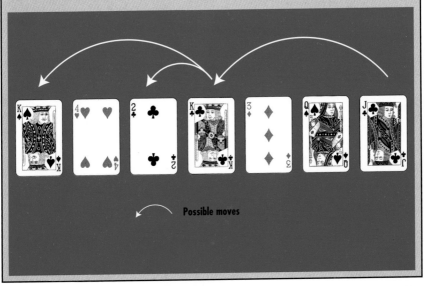

Possible moves

Castles in Spain

AIM OF THE GAME: To build up suits, in sequence, from the foundation cards.

HOW TO PLAY: Shuffle and cut a 52-card pack. Deal a row of five cards, laying them face down from left to right. Above this row lay a row of four cards, then a row of three above that. Finally place one card above the centre card of the row of three. Then lay down two further sets, also face down, on top of the first set.

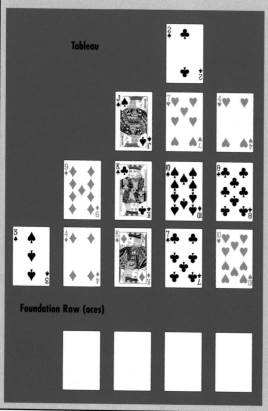

You have 13 cards left. Lay them face up, one by one, on top of the existing piles, keeping to the pattern. This makes 13 depot piles.

Any aces showing are played to the Foundation Row, once the Tableau is set out. The card beneath the ace is turned up and becomes available for play. Available cards may be played either on to their foundation pile, or in descending sequence of alternate colour on another depot pile.

Sequences or part sequences may be moved from one depot pile to another or to fill any spaces that are created. The cards may not be redealt.

Klondike

AIM OF THE GAME: To build each foundation card in suit and sequence, ace (low) to king.

HOW TO PLAY: Use the standard 52-card pack. Deal one card face up and six others face down in a single row, left to right.

Deal a card face up on top of the second card, then five face down on top of the others. Deal a card face up on the third pile, and another four face down, and continue in this way until you have seven piles as shown below. The remaining cards (the stock) are placed in a packet, face down. Aces are the foundation cards and should be placed in a row of four, separate from the seven piles, as you find them. Within the layout, you want to build sequences of alternating colours, e.g. a red six on a black seven, black seven on red eight with the king at the base of the pile.

Cards can be transferred to their foundation piles, but cannot be moved again. All face-up cards on a pile in the layout must be moved as a unit. Whenever a card, or set of cards, is moved from one file to another, the face-down card that was beneath is turned over to become available. When a space is made in the layout, it can only be filled by a king. The top card of the stock (kept face down) is always available. If the card from stock is not useable, it goes into the talon, face up. When the stock is used up, the talon can be turned over and used as stock, but only once.

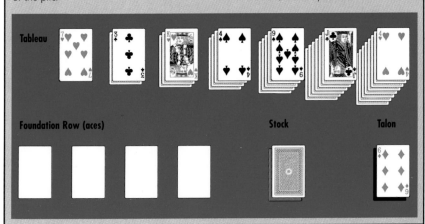

Tableau

Foundation Row (aces)   Stock   Talon

Golf

AIM OF THE GAME: To completely clear the tableau.

HOW TO PLAY: Use the standard 52-card pack. Deal a row of seven cards, face up. Then deal four more rows face up on the first row, making a total of 35 cards, arranged so that all card values can be easily seen.

Turn up the first card from the hand and lay it down face up to form the talon.
Any card from the top layer of the tableau pile can be removed and placed on the talon, so long as it is in numerical sequence with the top card, whether upwards or downwards.

Cards are turned up from the hand, or stock, and placed on the talon.

Cards in sequence may be played off the tableau on to the talon, so long as each pair of cards is in sequence, upwards or downwards. Suits do not matter.

Laying down a king stops the sequence. Aces are low and only a two may be placed on top of an ace.

The game is won if the tableau can be completely cleared on to the talon.

Why 'Golf'? You can score the game by treating each deal as a golf hole. Each card remaining in your tableau at the end of a deal counts as a stroke. Par is a total of 36 in nine deals. If the tableau is cleared, any cards remaining in the stock count as one minus-stroke each, and are deducted from the running total.

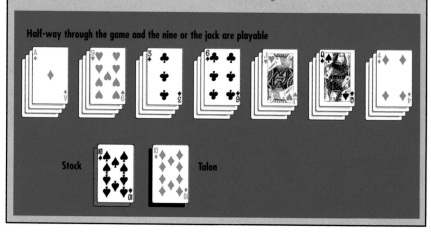

Half-way through the game and the nine or the jack are playable

Stock

Talon

Canfield

AIM OF THE GAME: To complete the foundations and tableau.

HOW TO PLAY: With the 52-card pack, deal 13 cards face down in one pile, turn the pile face up and place it at your left to form the stock. Deal the 14th card face-up and place it above and to the right of the stock pile. This is the first foundation card.

Deal four more cards face up in a row to the right of the stock, with the first card directly under the first foundation card. These form the tableau. The other three foundation cards are the other cards of the same pip value as the first one. Place them next to the first, face up, as they are turned up. The 34 cards remaining are placed face down, below the tableau. This is the hand. The top three cards are turned over and laid alongside the hand. Only the top card of these three is available. If playable, it can be played on to a foundation pile or on to the tableau, and the card beneath becomes available. If not playable, it is the first card of the waste pile or talon. Once all possible cards are played, three more are turned over and placed on top of the talon. When the hand is exhausted, the talon is turned over, without being shuffled, and becomes the new hand. This can be repeated indefinitely. Foundation piles are built up in suit sequence from the foundation card (e.g. 7, 8, 9, 10, J, Q, K, A, 2, 3, 4, 5, 6). Tableau piles are built up in the sequence of next lowest rank and opposite colour (black seven on top of red eight). A tableau pile is moved only as a unit, on to a card of next highest rank and opposite colour to the bottom card of the unit. Spaces occurring in the tableau must be filled from the top of the stock, or from the top of the talon if the stock is used up.

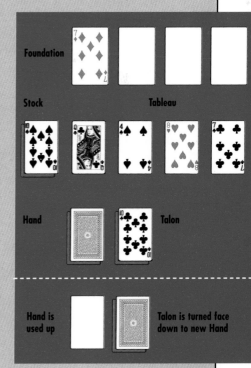

Tower of Pisa

AIM OF THE GAME: To finish with a single file of cards descending in sequence from ten to two.

HOW TO PLAY: From a full 52-card pack, remove a total of nine number cards, making a complete sequence from ten to two, in any mixture of suits. Lay them out in three columns of three. Discard the rest of the pack – it is not required. Once this is done, you can move cards.

Only the bottom card of a column can be moved, and it can only be moved to the bottom of another column, and under a card of higher value. An empty file can be filled by the bottom card of either of the other two files.

Helpful Hint: If you start with a ten on the bottom row, try to use all the cards from one of the files, creating an empty file in which you can then move the ten to the top (so long as it is still at the bottom of its file after your previous moves).

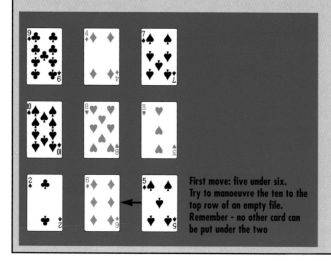

**First move: five under six.
Try to manoeuvre the ten to the
top row of an empty file.
Remember - no other card can
be put under the two**

Clock Patience

AIM OF THE GAME: To arrange all of the cards in a clock-face formation, with the kings in the centre.

HOW TO PLAY: Use the standard 52-card pack. Deal out 13 packets of four cards, face down. Place 12 of the packets in a circular formation, like the numbers on a clock face. Place the 13th packet in the centre of the 'clock' to form the stock pile. Turn the top card of the stock pile face up.

If it is a queen, it counts as 12; if a jack, as 11; if an ace, as one. Other cards have numbers corresponding to their pip values, and your aim is to have them all at the right place on the 'clock': e.g. all four sixes at six o'clock and all queens at twelve o'clock.

Place the turned-up card in the right place on the clock face, under the packet, face up; turn over the top card of that packet. Place that card in its right place in the same manner; turn over the top card of that packet, and so on.

If you turn over a king, place him face up at the bottom of the stock pile, and turn over the top card on the stock pile.

Continue until all four kings have been turned up and placed in the stock pile. You win if the last card to be turned up is the fourth king, because by then you will have completed the clock.

If the face-up card on the stock is a two it goes to the two o'clock (under the packet, face up)

Turn over top card. Place it face-up under the packet at eleven o'clock and carry on

Shamrocks

AIM OF THE GAME: To assemble complete suit sequences from ace to king, on the foundation piles.

HOW TO PLAY: Use the standard 52-card pack. Deal all the cards into 17 sets of three, spread out in fan shapes so that suit and pip value are clearly seen. There will be one card left. This too goes face up on the layout.

Only the fully exposed cards are available

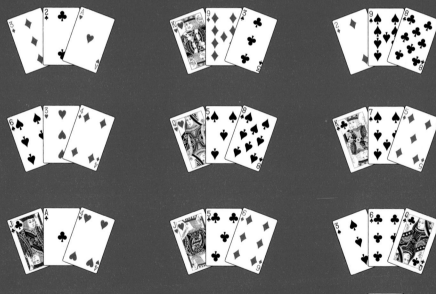

First move is on to the single card

If you have a king and another card of the same suit in one of your fans, put the king below the other.

Uncovered cards are available for play. The first move must be to add a card to the single card. No fan is allowed to hold more than three cards. As they appear, aces should be moved beyond the layout, in a row of four, to form the bases of foundation piles.

When you have moved all the cards from a fan, the space remains empty.

Foundation Row (aces)

Games for Two

Many card games can be played by different
numbers of people. Some, like Beggar
Your Neighbour (see page 21), can be played
by two to eight people. Even then, most games
have an ideal number of players, which suits the
game best. But for times when only two can
play, here is a selection of games that
work very well for two players.

Beggar Your Neighbour

AIM OF THE GAME: To win all 52 cards.

HOW TO PLAY: Use the standard pack of 52 cards. Cut for dealer (higher card). The non-dealer shuffles the cards. Each receives 26 cards.

The cards should be set out in a pile, face down. Each player turns over the top card and places it in front of his pile. The higher card wins the other (aces are low), and the player takes both cards and puts them face down. If two cards of the same value are turned over, then a 'war' is declared. The two equal cards are placed in the centre of the table. Each player makes a pile of three cards placed face down, with a fourth on top, face up. The higher of the face-up cards wins both piles, plus the two cards in the centre. If the two face-up cards are of equal value, the war is repeated, and the winner takes all the cards played. The game goes on until one player has all the cards.

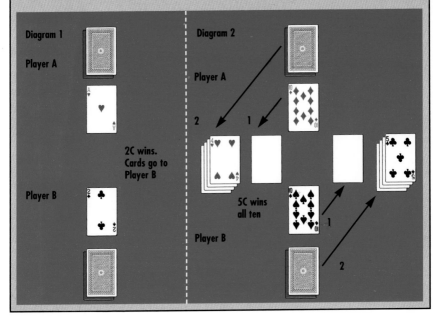

Diagram 1

Player A

2C wins.
Cards go to
Player B

Player B

Diagram 2

Player A

2   1

5C wins
all ten

1

Player B

2

21

Go Boom!

AIM OF THE GAME: To be first to get rid of all one's cards.

NUMBER OF PLAYERS: Two is the minimum; it can be played by up to six.

HOW TO PLAY: Use the pack of 52 cards. Cut for dealer (higher card). The dealer deals seven cards, one at a time, to each player. The rest of the pack is placed face down and forms the stock.

The player to the dealer's left leads. Other players must follow suit, or play a card of the same face value as the lead (aces are high). A player who has no playable card must draw from the stock until he receives a playable card. Once the stock is used up, players with no playable cards must wait for the next trick to be played (i.e. they pass). The trick is won by the highest card of the suit led. The winner of a trick leads to the next trick. Tricks are put into a discard pile since they have no score value.

The first player to have no cards left is the one who 'Goes Boom!' and wins the game.

Lead card

No playable card. Draw from stock

1

You can play 10S or 4D

2

Old Maid

AIM OF THE GAME: To avoid being left holding the last queen.

NUMBER OF PLAYERS: Minimum of two, though many more can play.

HOW TO PLAY: Cut for dealer (higher card). Set aside the queen of clubs from a 52-card pack, and deal out the remaining 51 cards (one player will have an extra card).

Each player's cards are spread out, face up, and any pairs are removed and placed face up in the centre of the table. The rest of each hand is then shuffled, and the player holding the unpaired queen holds his hand up, cards hidden, for the opponent to draw a card from. If the drawn card makes a pair, the pair is discarded. It is then the opponent's turn to shuffle and offer the cards. Eventually, all the cards will be paired except for the one remaining queen – the old maid – and whoever is left with it loses the round. Play can go on for an agreed number of rounds, with the winner taking the most rounds.

Pelmanism (or Memory)

AIM OF THE GAME: To collect all, or most, of the cards.

NUMBER OF PLAYERS: Up to six can play, but two is best.

HOW TO PLAY: Cut the cards to determine who goes first (higher card). Spread out the entire pack (52 cards) face down, leaving space between each card.

The first player turns over any two cards. If they make a pair (same number or rank), he takes them out and stacks them in front of him. He then turns over two more, until he fails to make a pair. The cards that do not make a pair are returned face down to their original position, and the turn passes to the other player. The game continues until all the cards have been picked up: the player with the greatest number of tricks (pairs) is the winner.

HELPFUL HINT: A geographical memory is needed to win this game – try to remember the positions of the cards which have been turned up and then turned face down again.

Frogs in the Pond

AIM OF THE GAME: To be first to score 100 points, by winning tricks.

HOW TO PLAY: Use the 52-card pack. Cut for dealer (higher card). The dealer deals ten
cards to each, two at a time. He then deals ten cards face down in the centre of the
table: the 'frogs in the pond'.

The dealer leads a single card. The
opponent must follow suit, from his ten
cards; if he cannot, the penalty is ten points,
and the dealer takes the trick. Alternatively,
the opponent follows suit and wins
ten points.

The winner of each trick takes the cards
played, plus one frog, which goes face
down on the trick gained. The winner then
leads for the next trick.

There are no trumps. Players keep the
tricks they have won. When all cards have

been played, the score – including frogs – is
added up, and another round begins.

SCORING: Only certain cards have value:
tens, 10; fives, 5; aces, 4; kings,
3; queens, 2; jacks, 1; others, nil.

Note: In the basic version, you only have to
follow suit to win the trick, even if you play
a lower card. It is also possible to play so
that the higher card in the led suit wins
the trick.

Lead card

First trick won
by your
opponent

Frogs

Play KH to take
the trick

German Whist

This is the best form of Whist for two players.

AIM OF THE GAME: To build a winning hand and score 50 points.

HOW TO PLAY: Use the 52-card pack. Cut for dealer (higher card). Dealer then deals 13 cards alternately to each player. The 27th card is turned over to denote trumps. The remainder forms the stock, face down.

The dealer leads a card, and the opponent can either beat it with a higher card of the same suit, or any trump (if trumps were not played), or he can play a lower card and lose the trick.

The winner of the first trick takes the face-up trump card, waits for his opponent to draw a fresh card from the stock, then turns over the next card.

The game continues until all the stock has been played: this marks the end of the first stage.

In the second stage, the players' hands are played out, with the winner of the last trick of the first stage taking the lead.

HELPFUL HINT: In the first stage of the game, it is vital to build up a strong hand in anticipation of the second stage.

SCORING: One point per trick. Target score is normally 50, although this can be varied by agreement among the players.

Your hand

Arrange cards by suit and value – HCDS.
Diamonds are your long suit. In the first stage, try to strike a balance between collecting high cards and winning tricks, but in the second phase try to exploit any trumps you have to best advantage

Racing Demon

AIM OF THE GAME: To be first to get rid of your demon pile, and to score 200 points.

HOW TO PLAY: Two 52-card packs are needed, with backs of different pattern or colour: one pack for each player. Each player deals 13 cards face down into a pile – these are the demon piles.

The top card of each demon pile is turned over. Each player then deals a further four cards from his stock, placing them individually in a row to the right of the demon pile. These make the bases of foundation piles and can be built on in descending order of alternate colours (e.g. black five, red four, black three and so on). Cards can be added from the stock or from the turned-up demon cards.

Cards from the stock piles are turned up in sets of three; a card that cannot be used goes into a discard pile which becomes the stock once the original stock is exhausted.

As aces become available, they are placed face up, separately, forming eight piles in the centre of the table within reach of both players and upon which either player can build in upwards sequence, treating the ace as low. Cards can be transferred to these piles, but must then remain there.

SCORING: The winner of a round scores ten points. Each player scores one point for every card played (i.e. not in the demon pile, the stock or the discard pile). The player with cards left in his demon pile doubles their value and subtracts this from his total of played cards. If kings are placed on the foundation piles, an extra ten points should be awarded for each king.

Sample set-up (one player)

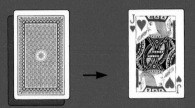

Discard Pile

Foundation Piles

Demon Pile (13 cards)

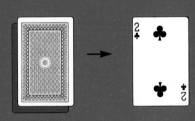 

Ace Piles

Seven-Up

This game used to be known in Britain as All-Fours.

AIM OF THE GAME: To be first to reach seven points, by building up a trick-winning hand.

HOW TO PLAY: Use a 52-card pack. Draw for dealer – the higher card wins. Dealer deals six cards to each player, in two sets of three. The top card of the stock is then turned over to determine trumps. If a jack is turned up, the dealer gets one point.

The other player begins, by either standing (accepting the turned-up card as trumps) or begging (requesting a different suit). The dealer can accept or deny this request. If he accepts it, he deals three new cards to each and turns over the new top card of the stock, until a trump is agreed. If the dealer refuses to change trumps, the other player scores one point, and play continues.

Each player, if necessary, discards enough of his cards to reduce his hand to six. The non-dealer leads, placing a card face up. The dealer must follow suit, with a higher value, or play a trump to win the trick. Otherwise the trick is awarded to the other player. The winner of the trick leads the next card.

SCORING: Single points are won as follows:

HIGH: The player dealt the highest trump in play.

LOW: The player dealt the lowest trump in play.

JACK: The player winning the jack of trumps in a trick (unless the dealer turned it over to determine trumps).

GAME: The player with the highest total of point values for cards won in tricks. Values are: ace, 4; king, 3, queen, 2, jack, 1, ten, 10. No other cards have any value. If only one trump card is played, it collects two points, or three if it is the jack.

Stock

Trump

Your hand

1

Advice: Stand

Your hand

2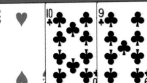

Advice: Beg

Gin Rummy

This is one of the many variations of Rummy.

AIM OF THE GAME: To build up a winning hand of melds (see Technical Terms page 8) and be first to score 100 points.

HOW TO PLAY: Cut for dealer, using the standard 52-card pack (aces high). Dealer shuffles, and deals ten cards to each player. The remaining cards, face down, form the stock. The top card is turned face up and placed by itself, to start the discard pile.

The other player has the option of taking that card or refusing it; he cannot draw a card from the stock pile. If he refuses it, the turn passes to the dealer. If the dealer also passes (refuses the turned-up card), the other player may take the top (face-down) card from stock. When a card is picked up, another must be placed on the discard pile.

The aim is to be the first to lay down all your cards in melds (sets of three or more cards of the same suit in consecutive numbers, counting from ace as low; or sets of three or more from different suits, but the same value).

If you have a full hand of melds, call out 'Gin!' You receive a bonus of 25 points plus the value of your opponent's unmelded cards. You can also choose to go out if you have some melds and the unmelded cards in your hand have a value of ten points or less, but if this is the case, then be careful because your opponent has the chance to complete his melds using your unmelded cards before the score is counted.

The player with the lower value of unmelded cards is awarded a bonus of 25 points.

If neither player has gone out before the last two cards are drawn from the stock, the round is treated as a no-score draw.

SCORING: Court cards (king, queen, jack): ten points each.
Ace: one point.
Number cards: as indicated by their pip value.
The value of the unmatched or unmelded cards still in your hand counts against you.
If the player who went out has the same, or greater, value of remaining cards as his opponent, the opponent receives a bonus of ten points together with the difference between the card values.
The winner of the game is the first player to reach 100 points.

Sample melds

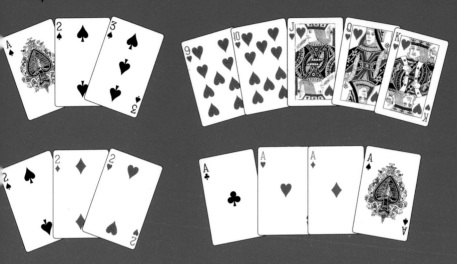

A dream hand

A hand from hell – no melds at all

Spoil Five

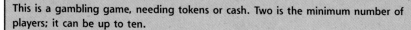

This is a gambling game, needing tokens or cash. Two is the minimum number of players; it can be up to ten.

AIM OF THE GAME: To win three or five tricks, or to stop the other player from doing so.

HOW TO PLAY: Use a pack of 52 cards. Each player puts an agreed number of tokens or coins in the pool. One player deals until a jack is dealt: the recipient of the jack becomes dealer, reshuffles, and deals for the game.

Hands of five are dealt, either two cards each and then three, or vice versa. Then the top card of the stock is turned over to determine trumps.

If it is an ace, the dealer may immediately pick it up and discard another card. If the other player is holding the ace of trumps, he passes a discard, face down, to the dealer, in exchange for the uncovered trump card. If the dealer holds the ace of trumps, he discards under the stock, on his turn, and picks up the turned-up trump.

The non-dealer makes the opening lead. The dealer must then follow suit or trump. If he is unable to follow suit or trump, any card may be played, but the trick will be lost. The trick is won by the highest card in the suit, or by the trump (or higher trump if trumps were led). The winner of the trick leads the next card.

RENEGING is possible: if a low trump is led, and the other player is holding the five or jack of trumps, or the ace of hearts, he

may retain these and play another card. But if a trump card higher than any of his is played, he must play the same suit (see Ranking Structure, page 33).

If neither player wins three tricks, the game is 'spoiled'. The dealing switches to the other player, more tokens go in the pool, and the game resumes.

If a player wins three tricks, he wins the pool. If he takes the first three tricks in a row, he can either throw in his cards or say 'Jink'. This means he expects to win the two remaining tricks, and if he does so, the opponent must pay him an extra token. If he fails to win the two tricks, the pool stands and a new round begins.

HELPFUL HINT: This game is well named 'Spoil Five'. There are plenty of opportunities in the scoring and trumping system, especially through reneging, to scupper your opponent, even if there is absolutely no possibility of winning three tricks yourself.

RANKING STRUCTURE IN SPOIL FIVE:

Whatever the trump suit, the ace of hearts is always the third-highest trump card. The highest trump is always the five.

HEARTS: five, jack, ace, king, queen, ten, nine, eight, seven, six, four, three, two.

DIAMONDS: five, jack, queen of hearts, ace, king, queen, ten, nine, eight, seven, six, four, three, two.

CLUBS and SPADES: as with diamonds. In non-trump suits, the ranking is different for the red and black suits:

HEARTS: ace, king, queen, jack, ten, nine, eight, seven, six, five, four, three, two.

DIAMONDS: As hearts, but with ace low.

CLUBS and SPADES: king, queen, jack, ace, two, three, four, five, six, seven, eight, nine, ten.

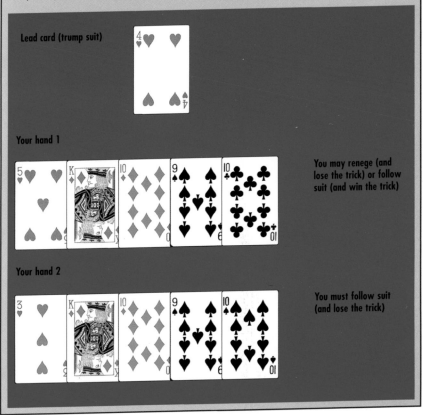

Lead card (trump suit)

Your hand 1

You may renege (and lose the trick) or follow suit (and win the trick)

Your hand 2

You must follow suit (and lose the trick)

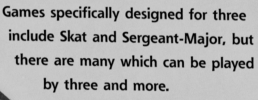

♥
♣ # Games for Three

Three is a very significant number in many
aspects of life. In cards, it is the minimum
number of players necessary to enable
players to combine in an alliance.
Games specifically designed for three
include Skat and Sergeant-Major, but
there are many which can be played
by three and more.

Crazy Eights Also known as 'Switch'.

AIM OF THE GAME: To be first to get rid of all one's cards, and to reach 500 points.

NUMBER OF PLAYERS: Can be played by two, but three to five is better.

HOW TO PLAY: Use the standard 52-card pack; two packs shuffled together if seven or more are playing. Cut for dealer (highest card). Dealer deals five cards to each player, from his left, one at a time. The stock goes face down, with the top card turned face up and laid alongside to start the discard pile.

Starting with the player on the dealer's left, each player either puts down a playable card face up on the discard pile, or draws a card from stock. Playable cards depend on the top card on the discard pile. If it is not an eight, any card may be played which matches the suit or is equal in value. If it is an eight, then any card of the same suit may be played. An eight may be played at any time, and the player who leads it can name the suit that must be played next. The first player to go out calls 'Crazy Eights!' and wins the round. First player to reach 500 points wins the game.

SCORING: The winner scores 100. Penalty scores for players with cards in hand are as follows:
Eight: 50
Court card: 10
Other cards: face value

Stock Pile

1

Discard Pile

Any diamond may be played on to the discard pile; or any eight

Stock Pile

2

Any diamond, queen or eight may be played on to the discard pile

VARIANTS: A player who is down to one card must knock to indicate this, or else pick up two cards from the stock. If the player before you puts down a queen, you miss that turn. When an ace is played, reverse the direction of play. If a two or a five of any suit is played, the next player must pick up two or five cards accordingly.

Knaves

AIM OF THE GAME: To win the greatest number of tricks, without taking any jacks (knaves).

HOW TO PLAY: Use the 52-card pack. Cut for dealer (highest card). The dealer deals 17 cards to each player, one card at a time. The remaining card is turned over to denote trumps for the round.

The player to the dealer's left leads by laying down a card. Other players must follow suit, trump, or discard a card. Continue until all cards are played.

SCORING: Each trick won receives one point. The first player to reach 20 points wins the game. But any trick containing a jack is penalized by deducting points as follows: jack of hearts, four; diamonds, three; clubs, two; spades, one.

HELPFUL HINT: If you hold a jack, don't lead with it, or your opponents may force you to win the trick, and so lose points.

REVOKING: This is failing to follow suit in a trick when you are able to. If you correct the error before the trick is turned over, there is no penalty. If you are caught – although only before the start of the next trick – you cannot win the trick, and you incur a three-point penalty.

Penalty points for jacks

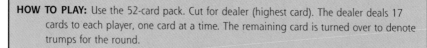

Sevens

AIM OF THE GAME: To get rid of all your cards.

NUMBER OF PLAYERS: Three to eight.

HOW TO PLAY: This is a gambling game, so each player starts off with an equal number of chips, and puts a chip into the pool at the start.

Use the pack of 52 cards. Choose the dealer by someone dealing cards face up; the first to get a jack becomes the dealer. The dealer shuffles, and the player to his right cuts.

Cards are dealt one at a time, from the dealer's left, until the pack is used up.

Play begins from the dealer's left. The first card to be played must be a seven. If you have no seven, you pass, and pay a chip to the pool.

When a seven is put down, the six and eight of the same suit are also available for play, and once these are down, the next values above and below can be played.

The four sevens are laid in a row in the centre of the table, with the sixes to one side and the eights to the other. Suits can then be built up to the king and down to the ace, which is low.

Only one card can be played in each turn. If you can play a card, you must. If you pass when able to play, pay a penalty of three chips to the pool.

The first player to lay down all his cards wins. Others pay one chip for each card

they are left holding, and the winner then takes the whole pool.

HELPFUL HINT: It's almost always best to play from your 'long suit' – the suit you have most cards in.

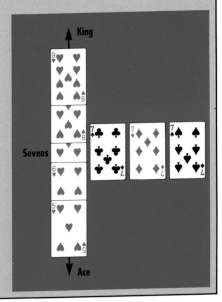

Knock-Out Whist

AIM OF THE GAME: To win the greatest number of tricks.

HOW TO PLAY: Use the 52-card pack. Cut for dealer (highest card). The dealer then deals seven cards to each player. The rest of the cards are placed face down, but the top one is turned over to determine trumps.

The player to the dealer's left leads the first card. Players must follow suit if they can, otherwise they may play any card.

In the second round, six cards are dealt (and five in the third round, down to one in the final round). The winner of a round calls trumps for the next, after the deal.

In the seventh round, when only one card is dealt to each player, the players should cut for trumps.

A player who takes no tricks in any round is 'knocked' out and takes no more part in the game. However, the first player to take no tricks is awarded the 'dog's chance'. He is dealt one card in the next round, and can play it to the trick of his choice. If he does

not play it to a particular trick, he knocks on the table, and play passes to the next in turn. If he wins a trick, he is fully back in the game for the next round.

The game can be won in any round after the third if one player takes all the tricks.

HELPFUL HINT: When choosing trumps, look for the longest suit (i.e. most cards of the same suit) that you have, rather than the highest-value cards, which might well win tricks on their own anyway. Also, after the third, try to trump high-value cards, because this should reduce the number of tricks your opposition will be able to win. If you must discard, discard a certain loser.

Sample hand

You call for trumps – go for diamonds, your long suit

Cheat

AIM OF THE GAME: To be first to get rid of all the cards in your hand.

NUMBER OF PLAYERS: Three or more.

HOW TO PLAY: Use the 52-pack. Cut for dealer (higest card wins). The dealer deals all the cards, one at a time.

The player to the dealer's left leads, by placing face down one or more cards. He says what the cards are – but he may be lying about the number of cards, their suit and their value.

An opposing player may call 'Cheat!' at any point. The last player has then to turn his discards face up. If he was cheating, he has to pick up all the cards in the discard pile. If he was not cheating, the caller must take all the discards.

If there is no call, the next player to the left takes his turn, placing his cards face down on the cards already played. He can play only cards of the same value as those just announced, or the next rank up (ace if it was a king, two if it was an ace). But – he may cheat.

HELPFUL HINTS: This can be an uproarious game. But watch the other players' faces – and try to keep your own deadpan. When you say what cards you are leading, look sneaky when telling the truth, and sincere when cheating – or the other way about.

Always challenge a player who is going out – you have nothing to lose.

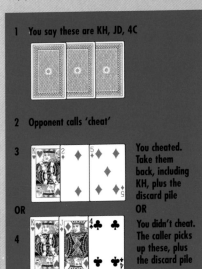

1 **You say these are KH, JD, 4C**

2 **Opponent calls 'cheat'**

3 You cheated. Take them back, including KH, plus the discard pile

OR

OR

4 You didn't cheat. The caller picks up these, plus the discard pile

Hearts

AIM OF THE GAME: To win tricks without winning any cards from the hearts suit.

NUMBER OF PLAYERS: From three to six.

HOW TO PLAY: Use the standard pack of 52, but with three players, take out the two of clubs. This equalizes the hands. Cut for dealer (lowest card). Dealing goes to the left. All cards should be dealt out, one at a time.

The opening lead is made by the player on the dealer's left. Other players must follow suit if they can, otherwise any card may be played. There are no trumps. The highest card of the leading suit wins. The winning player leads to the next trick.

SCORING: The aim is to avoid collecting hearts and to lose any that one is dealt. Each time a player takes a heart, he loses a point.
At the end of the round, each player adds his score of hearts, adding one for each heart card he has. The lowest score wins the round. The game continues until one player reaches a score of 30. The player with the lowest score is the winner.

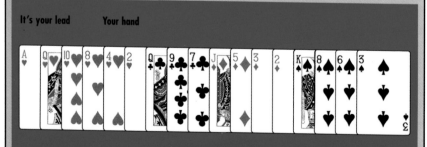

It's your lead   Your hand

Who shuffled this lot? Keep your hearts in the hope that you can lose them when you can't follow suit. Play your KS or QC, and hope you won't pick up any more hearts

VARIANT 1: When three are playing, add the joker to the pack and subtract the two of clubs and two of diamonds, allowing each player to receive 17 cards. The joker makes an additional heart between the ten and the jack.

VARIANT 2: The queen of spades is an additional heart, but she scores 20 points if won. The ace of hearts scores 15, the court hearts score 10, and the other hearts score their pip value. Additionally, the heart cards are all trumps, although the queen of spades is not. In this version, the worst possible score in a hand is 120.

In this version, the game ends when someone reaches a total point score of 500. The player with the lowest score wins.

VARIANT 3: You can add further to the excitement by introducing a bonus card into the game. This is usually the jack of diamonds, and he counts for 20 plus-points, offsetting 'Black Maria', the queen of spades.

Dealt a hand like this, with the lead, play your high diamonds first so that you can discard your high spades when diamonds are next played. If you haven't the lead, try and win it as soon as possible so that you can direct the game towards shortening diamonds.

What a lot of hearts – but remember: they are all trumps. If you play them well – and you can afford to start with the lowest ones – then your bonus card could end up putting you nicely ahead

Sergeant-Major

A gambling game using tokens or agreed cash values for each point.

AIM OF THE GAME: To win the greatest number of tricks from a single hand.

HOW TO PLAY: Use the pack of 52. Cut for dealer (highest card). The dealer deals 16 cards to each player. The last four cards are placed face down. These form the kitty.

The dealer selects trumps, and discards four of his cards, face down, then picks up the kitty to add to his hand.

The player to the dealer's left leads any card to the first trick. Other players must follow suit if they can, or trump, or discard. The trick is won by the highest card of the suit that led, or the highest trump.

Each player has a target to meet. The dealer's is eight, the player's to his left is five; the third player's is three.

At the end of the round, after scoring, the deal moves to the left. When the new deal is dealt, each player who was up in the previous round gives away one card of his choice for each extra trick to a down player, who must return the highest card he has of the same suit or suits. This can mean returning a card he has just been given.

The game ends when any player wins 12 or more tricks from one hand.

SCORING: A player beating the target is said to be up by the difference between his score and the target; a player short of target is said to be down by the same difference. The latter pay a token for each trick they are down; the former receive one for each extra trick.

Your hand

You are the dealer. Which four to discard? Remember you call trumps. Stay with your long suit.
Discard your four lowest non-club cards and hope to pick up four higher-value cards

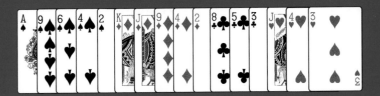

You are two up from the previous round, and clubs are trumps. Obviously, that wasn't your decision! Which cards will you exchange for (hopefully) higher values? Certainly three of hearts and probably the two of diamonds

A very strange distribution, and one not helped by the fact that you are three down and clubs are trumps. However, with no spades and length as well as strength in hearts, you might be able to play yourself out of the situation. Play hearts everytime you win a trick, and eventually, once all the trumps have been exhausted you might make the three and two of hearts!

You are one up from the previous round, you are the dealer, you have not swapped cards and now you must choose trumps. Which suit will you choose? In each suit you have four cards, and in each you have court cards. However, the strongest suit is diamonds, because they are in sequence and provide three clear winners despite the absence of the ace.

Skat

This is a simpler form of the famous German game 'Skat', also known in German as 'Schafkopf' (Sheep's Head).

AIM OF THE GAME: To be first to score ten game points.

NUMBER OF PLAYERS: Three.

HOW TO PLAY: Use a pack of 32 cards (ace, king, queen, jack, ten, nine, eight, seven in each suit). Cut for dealer (highest card). Dealer deals ten cards to each player, in sets of three-four-three at a time, and places the next two cards face down on the table. These are the skat (sometimes called the widow).

The player to the dealer's left is First Hand. He has first right to pick up the skat. The player on his left (Middle Hand) is next if First Hand passes, and the third is Last Hand. He can pick up the skat if Middle Hand passes. The first player to take the skat is called the Player. He discards two cards face down to replace the skat.

The Player contracts to win at least 61 points (see point values) in tricks taken. First Hand leads (he may or may not be the Player). The others must follow suit if they can; if not, any card may be played. A trick is won by the highest card of the suit led, or by the highest trump. The winner of the trick leads to the next. If all three players pass, the skat is set aside, and First Hand leads in the normal way. The skat is added to the cards of the player who wins the last trick. This way of playing the game is called Least, because now the aim is to win as few points in tricks as possible.

TRUMPS AND POINT VALUES: All queens and jacks and all diamonds are trumps. Ranking order of trumps is as follows: queens of clubs, spades, hearts, diamonds; then jacks in the same sequence of suits. Then come the other diamonds: ace, ten, king, nine, eight, seven. In the other suits, the ranking is: ace, ten, king, nine, eight, seven. Note that the ten outranks the king.

The point values are: ace, 11; ten, 10; king, 4; queen, 3; jack, 2; others, nil.

SCORING: 1. If the skat has been taken up: If the Player takes from 61 to 90 points, he scores two Game Points. If he takes 91 or more points, he scores four Game Points. This is known as making Schneider. If he takes all the tricks, he scores six Game Points, which is termed a Schwartz. At the end of play, the point values of his two discards are also counted in his favour. If the Player falls short of his contract to win 61 or more points, he loses two Game Points if his score is between 31 and 60; and four Game Points (Schneider) if his score is under 31. If he takes no tricks at all, he loses six Game Points (Schwartz).

2. If the skat was not taken up: If a player has no tricks, he scores four Game Points. If a player has taken all the tricks, he loses four Game Points. If each player has taken at least one trick, the one with the lowest point value scores two Game Points. If two players tie with the same lowest point value, the two Game Points go to the player who lost the last trick between the two. If each player scores 40 value points, the dealer is awarded the two Game Points.

HELPFUL HINT: With so many trump cards in the game, you should not take up the skat unless you are strong in trumps: say at least seven already in your hand.

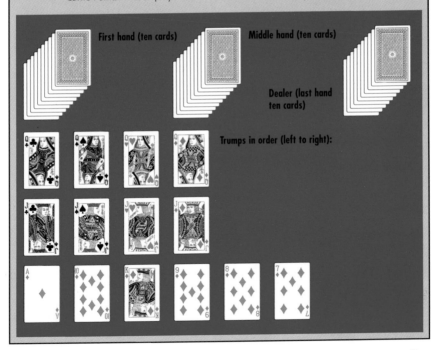

First hand (ten cards) Middle hand (ten cards)

Dealer (last hand ten cards)

Trumps in order (left to right):

Five Hundred

AIM OF THE GAME: To make, or beat, the contract; and be first to score 500 points.

NUMBER OF PLAYERS: Two to six, but three is the ideal number.

HOW TO PLAY: Use a pack of 32 cards (standard pack excluding all cards between two and six inclusive), plus a joker. Draw for first deal: lowest card wins (ace low, joker lowest).

Deal to the left, ten cards to each player in packets of three-four-three. After the first round of three, three cards are laid face down in the centre. This is the widow. Having seen their hands, each player may make a single bid, or pass. Each bid states the number of tricks the player will take, from six to ten, and his trump suit (or no trumps), e.g. 'eight diamonds'; 'ten no trumps'. Each bid must be for a higher number of tricks than the bid before, or the same number if ten. The highest bid, or first to bid ten, becomes the contract.

If no one makes a bid, the dealt cards are collected, shuffled and redealt by the next dealer (player to the dealer's left). Bidding then resumes.

The other two players combine in alliance to defeat the bidder, but they may not see each other's hands.

The bidder takes up the widow, then discards any three cards from his hand. He can lead with any card. The others must follow suit, if able; if unable, any card may be played. The trick is won by the highest trump, or highest card of the suit led. The

winner of the trick leads to the next trick.

If the bidder had called no trumps, then the only trump is the joker. The trick can only be won by the highest card of the suit led, unless the joker is played, when it wins.

If a player leads with the joker, he must declare the suit that the others must follow, if they can.

TRUMPS: The ranking of suits, high to low, is: hearts, diamonds, clubs, spades. But a no trump bid outranks them all.

Card ranking in the trump suit: joker; jack; jack of the other suit of the same colour; ace; king; queen; ten; nine; eight; seven.

Card ranking in the non-trump suits: ace, king, queen, jack (but see above); ten; nine; eight; seven.

SCORING: Each player keeps a running total from round to round. The bidder's opponents keep their scores separately. See the table for the number of points awarded.

If the bidder makes his contract,

he scores the value of his bid. If his bid added up to less than 250, and he actually takes all ten tricks, he is awarded only 250. If he is set back (fails to make his contract), then the value of his bid is subtracted from his running total. This can produce a minus figure. Each opponent scores ten points for every trick he wins.

Game is made at 500. If another player goes out (hits 500) on the same deal as the bidder, the bidder wins.

VARIANT: A player may bid 'nullo'. This is an offer to win no tricks, at no trump. Its scoring value is 250, so its bid value is between eight clubs and eight spades. If the nullo bidder gains the contract, he loses if he wins a single trick. Each of his opponents gains ten points for each trick made by the bidder.

NUMBER OF TRICKS BID

	6	7	8	9	10
No trump	120	220	320	420	520
Hearts	100	200	300	400	500
Diamonds	80	180	280	380	480
Clubs	60	160	260	360	460
Spades	40	140	240	340	440

A hand for a 'no trumps' bid

A hand for a 'nullo' bid – but remember, you may pick up the joker from the window.

Games for Four or More

Exactly four is the number needed to play the classic versions of some of the best-known games, including Whist and Bridge, when two sets of partners play against each other. Apart from the excitement of sharing the game – and of trying to read your partner's mind or expression, since you don't see his cards – partnerships have the advantage of sharing the risk if you are playing for stakes. This section also includes a range of games which can be played by more than four, including Pontoon and Poker.

Authors

AIM OF THE GAME: To collect the most 'books', i.e. sets of four cards all of which have the same rank.

NUMBER OF PLAYERS: From three to six, but four or five make the best number.

HOW TO PLAY: Use the 52-card pack. Cut for dealer (highest card). The dealer deals out the full pack among the players; some may end up with a card less than others.

Play starts with the player to the left of the dealer. Looking at his hand, he decides what card to ask for. It must be of a rank in which he already has at least one card, from a different suit. He then chooses an opponent and addresses him by name, e.g. 'Dean, please give me the seven of hearts'.

If the opponent has that card, he must hand it over, and the asker's turn goes on until he asks for a card which an opponent does not have. The turn then passes to the player on his left. When a player has all four cards of the same rank, he lays them face down on the table, as a book. The winner is the one with most books.

If playing for stakes, the winner of each book collects a token from the other players. If a player asks for a card he already holds, or does not pass over a requested card when he has it, he pays a token to each other player.

HELPFUL HINT: Memory helps in this game; what a player asks for is also a clue as to what he has in his hand.

A book of jacks worth one token

Red Dog

A straightforward gambling game, with shifting odds.

AIM OF THE GAME: To guess correctly whether you can beat the pool.

NUMBER OF PLAYERS: From three upwards, but four upwards is preferable.

HOW TO PLAY: Each player puts an agreed amount of tokens or cash into the pool.

Use the 52-card pack. Cut for dealer (highest card). The dealer deals five cards to each player, or four if the number of players is nine or more. The stock is placed face down in front of the dealer.

The player to the dealer's left, having looked at his hand, bets anything from one unit to the whole pool that he holds a higher card of the same suit as the (unseen) top card on top of the stock. He must place his tokens or coins alongside the pool.

The dealer turns the top card over. If the player can produce a higher card of the same suit, then the dealer returns his stake and pays him from the pool. If the player loses, his bet goes into the pool and he shows his whole hand, face up, after which it is discarded for the next deal, and play passes to the next player on the left.

A player can pass (not offer a bet), but must pay one token to the pool.

If a player wins the whole pool, then each player contributes an equal amount to form a new pool and restart the game. If a player leaves the game, the pool must be equally divided and the game restarted.

HELPFUL HINT: Despite its simplicity, there is strategy in this game, especially if your turn comes towards the end. Watch what cards are turned over and shown: the odds are going in your favour all the time.

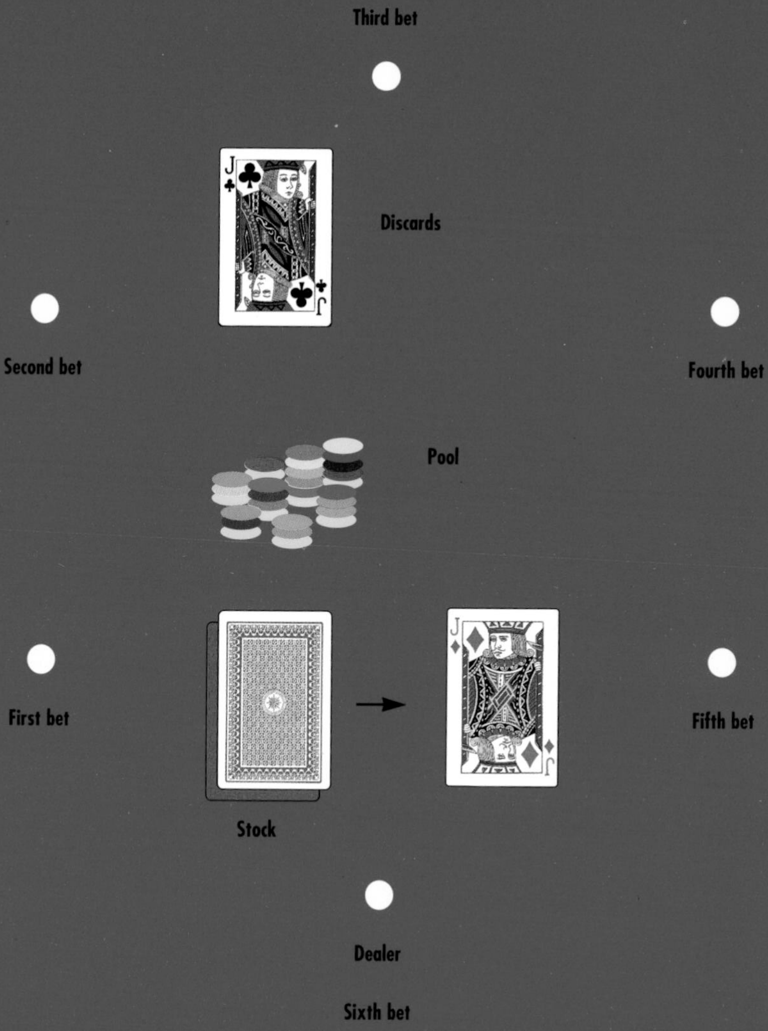

Third bet

J♣

Discards

Second bet

Fourth bet

Pool

First bet

Stock

→

J♦

Fifth bet

Dealer

Sixth bet

The top card of the stock is left face up and the next placed on top, and so on. Turn it over (without a reshuffle) if the stock pile is exhausted

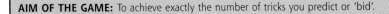

Oh Hell

A card game from the 1930s.

AIM OF THE GAME: To achieve exactly the number of tricks you predict or 'bid'.

NUMBER OF PLAYERS: From three to seven can play, but four is best.

HOW TO PLAY: Use the 52-card pack. Each player plays for himself alone; no partners. Cards are drawn: the highest is dealer and chooses where to sit. Others sit from the dealer's left in descending order of card drawn.

The first deal is one card each. Subsequent deals are increased by one card each until the 13th and last, when the full pack is dealt out (always in equal hands: remaining cards in the last deal are not used).

After each deal, except the last one, the next card is turned up to determine trumps. There are no trumps in the last deal.

Each player, starting from the dealer's left, must make a bid, i.e. predict the number of tricks he will take. This can include Zero, or Pass. Bids, also known as Contracts, are recorded on paper by a scorekeeper who, at the end of bidding, announces whether the total number of bids is over, under or even with the number of tricks that may be won in the round.

The player to the dealer's left leads. Other players must follow suit or, if unable to do so, may play any card including a trump. The winner of a trick leads to the next trick.

SCORING: A player who achieves his exact contract scores ten points plus the amount of his bid. A player who achieves either more or less than his bid 'busts' and receives no points.

HELPFUL HINT: If you find yourself busted in the course of the round, don't let on. This makes it harder for the others to read the game; if you are lucky, they will bust too.

Player C

Player B

Trump suit

Player D

Dealer

With the lead Player B could risk a bid. player C could certainly make a bid. Others would be well advised to pass unless player D is feeling particularly lucky

Fourth round

Player C

Player B

Trump suit

Player D

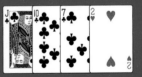

Dealer

Number of winable tricks: four
Player B bids two
Player C bids two
Player D bids one
Dealer bids one
Total is two bids over
Likely winner on this round is B.

Loo

The most common card game played in the gaming houses of England during the late 18th century.

AIM OF THE GAME: To win tricks.

NUMBER OF PLAYERS: From five to nine.

HOW TO PLAY: Use the standard pack of 52 cards. Aces are high. Players put an agreed number of tokens or coins into the pool. These must always be equally divisible by three.

Any player distributes cards until a jack is dealt: the recipient of the jack is first dealer. Trumps are not determined immediately. If all players are able to follow suit in each of the three leads, trumps are not called. But as soon as someone fails to follow suit, once that trick is completed, then the top card of the stock pile is turned face up to determine trumps for all remaining tricks.

Three cards are dealt, one at a time, to each player, starting to the dealer's left.

The player to the dealer's left leads. Others must follow suit if they can, otherwise they may trump (see above).

Tricks are not gathered together: the cards are left face up in front of the players.

SCORING: Each winning trick is entitled to win one third of the pool in each round. Players who have no tricks are looed. They must put a double stake into the pool for the next round.

VARIANT: The form of Loo described above is known as Single Pool. There is also Double Pool. In this, an extra hand, known as the miss, is dealt to the right of the dealer. The top card of the stock is turned up to determine trumps.

Before the opening lead, each player must tell the dealer whether he will stand, pass or take the miss.

To stand is to remain in play and participate in the tricks. To pass is to go out of play: the player's cards are placed face down under the stock. To take the miss is to pick up the extra hand and to place one's original hand face down under the stock. The player who does this cannot then pass; he must remain in play.

If all players pass except the dealer, or a player who has taken the miss, the lone player takes all the pool. If only one player ahead of the dealer stands, then the dealer must either stand, or take the miss, and 'defend' the pool.

In Double Pool, the leader for each trick must play a trump if he has one; and if he has the ace of trumps, that must be led first. If the ace was turned up and he has the king, then that must be led first.

SCORING: As before, each trick takes one third of the pool.

Where the dealer has had to defend the pool, he neither collects nor pays, but his opponent, depending on his score, does one or the other.

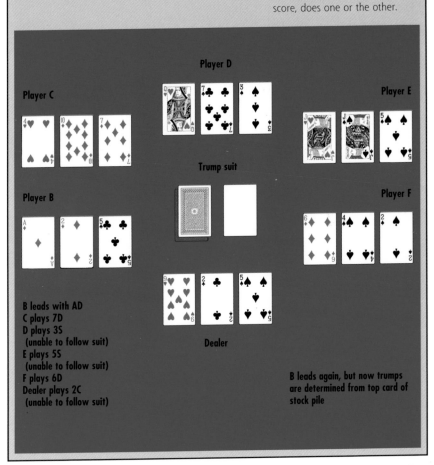

Player D

Player C

Player E

Trump suit

Player B

Player F

B leads with AD
C plays 7D
D plays 3S
 (unable to follow suit)
E plays 5S
 (unable to follow suit)
F plays 6D
Dealer plays 2C
 (unable to follow suit)

Dealer

B leads again, but now trumps are determined from top card of stock pile

Nap

The full name is 'Napoleon', and it is a gambling game, a member of the Euchre game group.

AIM OF THE GAME: As highest bidder, to win the contracted number of tricks.

NUMBER OF PLAYERS: From two to six, but four makes the best game.

HOW TO PLAY: Use the standard pack of 52 cards. Aces are high, except when drawing for the deal, when they are low. Lowest card is first to deal and has choice of seat, with second lowest on his left, and so on.

Players pay an agreed number of tokens or coins into the pool. The dealer deals out five cards, one at a time, to each player, starting on his left.

On receipt of the cards, each player, starting on the dealer's left, must make a bid for the number of tricks that he will win, if he can name the trump suit. Each must either bid higher than the previous bid, or pass. If all pass, the dealer must make the minimal bid of at least one trick. Otherwise the lowest acceptable bid is two. To bid for all five tricks is to go nap.

The highest bidder makes the opening lead, and the suit he leads becomes trumps. Others must follow suit if they can, or play a discard. The highest trump, or highest card of the leading suit in the next trick, wins. The winner leads to the next trick.

The other players set out to play against the highest bidder. If the highest bidder wins tricks over and above his bid, he receives no credit. As soon as he has won his forecast number of tricks, he must show his remaining cards to prove that he has not revoked at any point.

SCORING: If nap is made, it is worth ten points to the winner. If, having bid nap, the player fails to make it, he pays five points to the other players. If the player makes his bid, but it is less than nap, it is worth as many points as there are tricks; if he is defeated, he pays the same number of points to each of his opponents. Deals are settled at the end of each round.

HELPFUL HINTS: With only a part of the pack in play, the opportunities for bidding will be restricted, unless a very lucky hand is dealt. Even four assorted trumps, if they are not court cards, are only likely to win three tricks.

BIDDING MISERE. This is a bid that exceeds a bid for three tricks, but is itself exceeded by a bid for four. It offers an opportunity to a player with a poor hand, as it is a bid to take no tricks, on the basis of having no trumps.

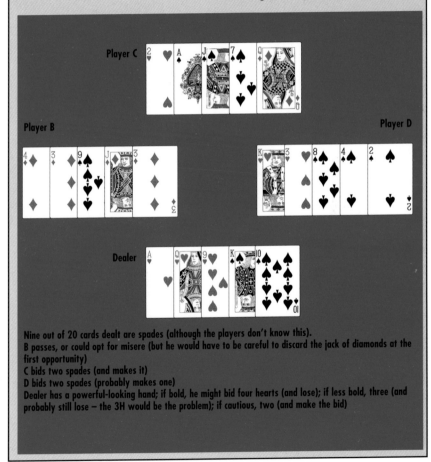

Nine out of 20 cards dealt are spades (although the players don't know this).

B passes, or could opt for misere (but he would have to be careful to discard the jack of diamonds at the first opportunity)

C bids two spades (and makes it)

D bids two spades (probably makes one)

Dealer has a powerful-looking hand; if bold, he might bid four hearts (and lose); if less bold, three (and probably still lose – the 3H would be the problem); if cautious, two (and make the bid)

Whist

This is one of the oldest card games, played for more than four hundred years. Familiarity with Whist makes a good introduction to the more complex game of Bridge, also played by two sets of partners.

AIM OF THE GAME: To take more tricks than the opposing partnership.

NUMBER OF PLAYERS: Four, playing as two sets of partners.

HOW TO PLAY: Use the pack of 52 cards. Normally two packs are employed, with different back designs or colours, so that one may be shuffled while the other is being dealt. Aces are high.

Players draw cards to decide partners, who sit facing each other across the table. The draw can be for the same suit or value. A draw is also made to find the dealer – highest card, with aces low.

The dealer deals out 13 cards to each player, one at a time, starting with the player to his left. The last card is turned face up to determine trumps: the dealer then adds it to his hand.

The player to the dealer's left leads. Others must follow suit if they can, otherwise trump or discard. The highest card of the led suit or a trump card wins. One partner from each side takes charge of the side's won tricks. The winner of a trick leads to the next trick.

SCORING: A partnership, or pair, has to take at least seven tricks to score. The first six tricks won have no scoring value. After the seventh, each trick counts for one point. Revoking is penalized by three points. The first side to gain five points wins the game. Points are also given for honour cards held. If a pair receive ace, king, queen and jack of the trump suit, they gain an extra four points. If they receive any three of the honour cards, they gain an extra two points. Points for honour cards are only given to a side which starts the deal with a score of less than four points.

Whist is normally played in a set of three games (a Rubber).

Unlike the other games in this book, Whist requires two partners to play together. They cannot show their hands to each other, nor give any information. Because of the follow-suit rule, opportunities for strategic play are fairly limited. But you need to watch your partner's lead very carefully. The normal lead is the fourth card in your longest suit. If you are not leading to make the trick, play low, to give your partner the chance to win it. This is the best way to conserve your high-value cards for winning later tricks.

Your hand

Your partner's hand (you don't see it)

Trumps are diamonds: not good for you, but not bad for your partner.
If it's your lead, lead 5H, this being the fourth highest card of your longest and strongest suit. If it was your partner's lead, he might play the 5D to draw out trumps. This would tell you that your partner has three higher trumps, plus, before his lead, five or more diamonds. Therefore you would know the balance of trumps is in your favour. If your partner keeps playing trumps, your opponents should run out of trumps by the third round of diamonds, leaving your partner with two 'free' trumps to play at any time. In the meantime, your opponents will have been trying to establish their longest and strongest suit. Whichever one they choose you have a block: the ace and king in hearts, the king and jack in clubs and the ace and queen in spades. Therefore, if you play this hand correctly you should make two, or even three, points.

Pontoon

Known in the USA as 'Blackjack', and in France as 'Vingt-et-Un' (Twenty-One), this is one of the best-known of gambling games. You will need to provide tokens or cash for betting.

AIM OF THE GAME: To form a hand whose total value is 21, or which beats the dealer's.

NUMBER OF PLAYERS: From two to eight or more, but five to eight is best.

CARD VALUES: Ace can count as one or 11 at the players' choice; kings, queens, jacks and tens all count as ten; other cards follow their pip value.

HOW TO PLAY: Use the 52-card pack (two packs shuffled together for more than eight). Cut for banker (highest card; he is also the dealer).

The banker deals one card to each player, going from his left and ending with himself. His card remains face down; everyone else picks up their card. Again from the banker's left, the players place their initial bets (between agreed maximum and minimum levels). The banker deals a second card face down to each player, and now all the players, including the banker, look at their two cards. If the banker has a Pontoon (ace – at 11 – plus a card scoring ten), he lays it down, face up. Each player has to pay double their stake to the banker, and the round ends. If the banker cannot declare a Pontoon, then each player from his left has a turn to improve their hand by acquiring extra cards. A player with a Pontoon declares it by placing it on the table, the ten face down and the ace face up on top of it. A player with two cards of equal value can split, by laying them face up on the table

and placing another stake equal to his first one. The banker deals another card, face down, to each of these. If again there are equal-value cards, there can be a further split. Each of these hands may then be played, one after the other, during the player's turn.

Note: if the cards are ten-point ones, they must be of the same nominal rank; two jacks may be split, but a jack and a king cannot.

If a player's cards total under 21, he can say 'I'll buy one'. He must bet again by the same amount as before, or up to double it. The banker then deals him another card face down. If the total is still under 21, he can buy again, once more increasing his stake. This time, any amount between the first bet and the second. If the total is still under 21, he can buy and bet again, in the same way. Instead of buying, if his total is under 21, a player can say 'Twist'. This means no increase in the stake, and the banker deals him another card face down. The player can then Twist again if his total is low, until he has up to five cards in his hand. Five cards totalling under 21 form a Five Card Trick. A player can buy and then twist, but not twist and then buy.

A player may decide to take no extra cards, and say 'Stick'. This is usual if his hand totals 15 or more. Play then passes to the next player on the left.

If at any time a player's hand exceeds 21, he is 'bust', and must throw in his hand, face up, and lose his stake to the bank. A player who is bust on one split hand can still play the other.

When the players have completed their turns, the banker turns his two cards face up. He can then add up to three extra cards, or stay with his hand.

At the end of the round, after scoring is completed, there are several possibilities: If no one had a Pontoon, the dealer adds all the used cards to the bottom of the pack and deals again, without shuffling. If there was a Pontoon, the cards are shuffled and cut before the next deal. The banker does not change unless he did not have a Pontoon, and another player did have one, without splitting his hand. That player takes over the bank. If two or more players are eligible, then the one nearest the banker's left becomes the new banker. A banker can also sell the bank to another player, after any round.

SCORING: If the banker has over 21, he is bust. He pays their stakes back to all players who have not also gone bust, with double to anyone with a Pontoon or a Five Card Trick. If the banker has 21 or less, with not more than four cards, he pays their stake back to any player with a higher hand value, and collects from those with an equal or lower value. A banker who stayed on 19 will say 'Paying 20'. All players then show their cards; those with 21 or a Five Card Trick receive double their stake. A banker with 21 pays only Pontoons and Five Card Tricks. If the banker has a Five Card Trick, he pays only Pontoons (double the stake). Every other player, even those with Five Card Tricks, pay double their stake to the banker.

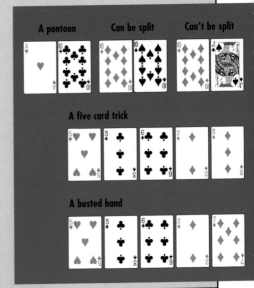

A pontoon   Can be split   Can't be split

A five card trick

A busted hand

Poker

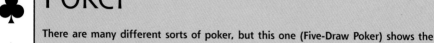

There are many different sorts of poker, but this one (Five-Draw Poker) shows the essential game.

AIM OF THE GAME: To have the highest-ranking hand at the end of the game.

NUMBER OF PLAYERS: Four or more.

HOW TO PLAY: Use the 52-card pack. Aces are high. The suits are all of equal value. The dealer is chosen by anyone dealing from a shuffled pack: first to get a jack becomes the first dealer. The cards are shuffled three times, lastly by the dealer, and the player to dealer's right cuts. Cards are dealt one at a time, from the dealer's left, until each player has five cards.

BETTING: Stakes should be agreed in advance (cash or chips). Each player antes a chip into the pool at the start. One player acts as Banker. Betting normally starts to the dealer's left and goes clockwise.

You can either call, raise or fold (sometimes called drop). If you fold, you discard your hand and lose your stake. If you call, you must put into the pool enough chips to match, but not exceed, what any other player has bet in that round. If you raise, you add more value to the call amount, subject to an agreed upper limit.

When you raise, you must say clearly the amount you are raising by.

Once everyone has made a bet, or folded, the remaining players discard up to three cards, and receive replacement cards from the dealer. Another betting round follows and you can again call, raise or fold. Previous bets cannot be withdrawn. At the end of each betting round, each player has to have put the same amount into the pool. If you don't do this, you have to fold.

Then hands are shown (the showdown). The highest hand wins the pot.

HELPFUL HINTS: Poker is a mix of luck and psychology. You have to watch your fellow players closely, and study their bets. If you hold a high hand, don't look too pleased or others will not raise the stakes and you will win less. If you have a low-scoring hand, fold unless you are feeling particularly lucky. If another player discards only one card, it's a danger signal – or a bluff. After all, this is the game that gave rise to the expression 'poker-face'.

SCORING

Poker hands consist of five cards. Each type of hand has a rank relative to the others – below is a list from highest ranked to lowest:

STRAIGHT FLUSH: Five cards in suit and sequence, ace being either high or low. A Royal Flush (ace-high straight flush) beats any other.

FOUR OF A KIND: Four cards of the same value (e.g. four kings or four twos), plus any other card.

FULL HOUSE: Three of one kind and a pair of another kind (e.g. three kings and two twos).

FLUSH: Five cards all of the same suit, but not in sequence.

STRAIGHT: Five cards in complete sequence of rank, ace either high or low, but of different suits.

THREE OF A KIND: Three cards of the same value, plus two others which are not a pair.

TWO PAIRS: Two sets of two of the same value, plus any other card.

PAIR: One set of two of the same value, plus any three other cards

HIGH CARD: Any hand which is not one of those listed above. If nobody has a Pair or better, then the highest card wins. If there is a tie for highest, then the next highest card wins.

Sample combinations

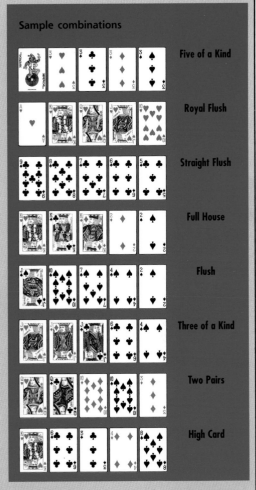

Five of a Kind

Royal Flush

Straight Flush

Full House

Flush

Three of a Kind

Two Pairs

High Card

VARIANT: Once you have mastered Five-Draw Poker, you can introduce Wild Cards, either by using a joker in the pack, or by naming another card as wild. With a joker, you can make a hand called Five of a Kind, which beats a Royal Flush (five aces is top, then five kings, etc.).

Index